NATIONAL GEOGRAPHIC

Ladders

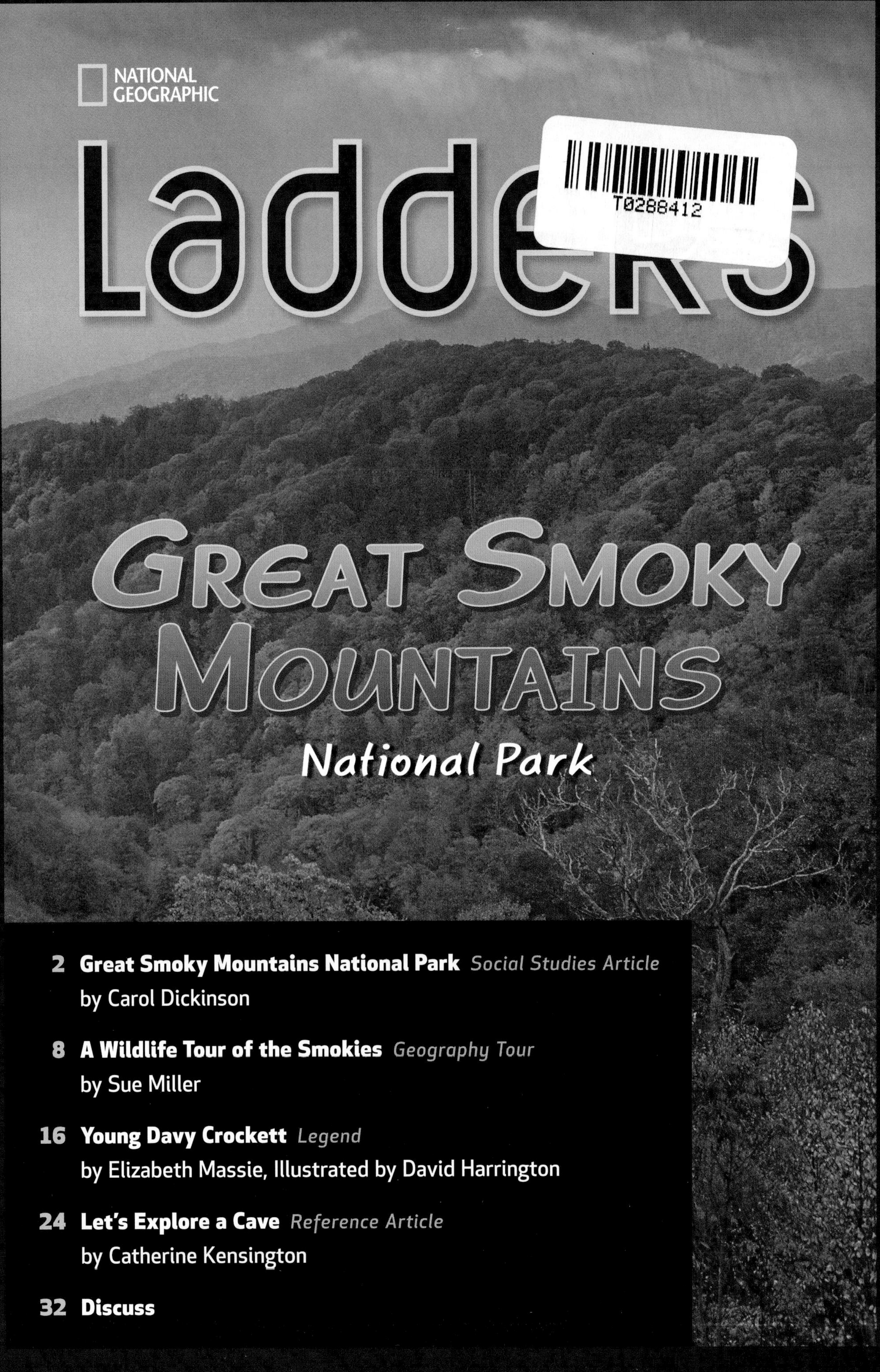

Great Smoky Mountains National Park

GENRE Social Studies Article

Read to find out how Great Smoky Mountains National Park came to exist.

Great Smoky Mountains National Park

by Carol Dickinson

Formed between 200 and 300 million years ago, the Great Smoky Mountains are some of the oldest mountains in the world. These mountains were 30,000 feet high or more. That's as high as 24 Empire State Buildings stacked one on top of the other. It is as high as most airplanes fly in the sky. Over millions of years, the Great Smoky Mountains **eroded**, or wore down, to their current height. These are still impressive mountains—at least 13 peaks stand higher than 5,000 feet.

The misty ridges of the Great Smoky Mountains gave the range its name.

People come from all around the world to enjoy the natural beauty of Great Smoky Mountains National Park, which lies on the border of North Carolina and Tennessee. They come to see the towering ridges, the rushing streams and rivers, and the plentiful wildlife. People camp beneath trees that are more than 100 years old. They hike the scenic Appalachian Trail that passes through the park on its way from Georgia to Maine.

1700s
Europeans begin settling near the Smoky Mountains. They share the land with the Cherokee, who have lived here for hundreds of years.

1786
Davy Crockett is born at the foot of the Smokies near Limestone, Tennessee. Crockett becomes an American hero.

1818
John Oliver settles his family in Cades Cove, which is now a part of the park. More European settlers follow. They found a small community in this mountain valley.

Get to Know the Park

Great Smoky Mountains National Park is one of the largest national parks east of the Rocky Mountains. The mountains are called "smoky" because of the blue mist that is often seen around the peaks. In fact, the Great Smoky Mountains are often just called "the Smokies."

The park was established in 1934 to protect mountain **habitats**, or places where animals live naturally, from people who wanted to cut down trees and put up buildings and towns. The Smokies provide safe habitats for many animals that live in mountain forests and meadows.

The park's highest peaks get an average of 85 inches of rain each year, and these heavy rains supply water for many miles of streams and rivers. The streams, forests, and meadows create an **ecosystem** where plants and animals live much as they did before people settled in the Smokies and began cutting down trees, hunting for food, and planting crops.

Among the wildlife that lives in the park's ecosystem are about 1,500 American black bears, and since the park was established, elk and otters have returned here to live in their natural habitats. They had been driven from this area when settlers arrived. The park is also home to many other animals, such as deer, wild turkeys, and hundreds of types of salamanders. As you can see, the park preserves a rich ecosystem that both the animals and park visitors can enjoy.

1900s

During the early 20th century, logging becomes a major industry in the Smokies. Many mountain forests are cut down.

1934

President Franklin D. Roosevelt signs an order officially establishing Great Smoky Mountains National Park.

2001

The park reintroduces American elk to the Smoky Mountains. Settlers and hunters had driven them out by the mid-1800s.

See those antlers? Male elk shed and regrow new antlers every year.

Take a Hike!

More people visit Great Smoky Mountains National Park each year than any other U.S. national park. They can create some crowded roads and traffic jams during summer and fall, the park's top seasons. Smart visitors park their cars and try out different forms of sightseeing. They rent bikes to ride on paved park roads or saddle up for a guided trip through the mountains on horseback. But in every season, hikers see the best of the Smokies as they walk through the park on foot.

Hikers who want to get a birds-eye view of the park should head up to Rocky Top, one of the three peaks of Thunderhead Mountain. Rocky Top lives up to its name—it's rocky. No trees or bushes grow there, so hikers who reach this peak can see ridge after ridge spread out before them. Below Rocky Top, the mountains are covered with forests, and from up here, you can see how important the forest habitats are to these mountains and the wildlife that lives here.

Because of their plentiful rain and steep slopes, the Great Smoky Mountains are famous for their mountain streams and waterfalls, and many park trails follow a stream to a waterfall. One of the most famous waterfalls in the park is also the highest. Ramsey Cascades tumbles 100 feet down a rocky slope and into a pool teeming with living things, including slippery salamanders. These little creatures are camouflage experts. Their coloring is so similar to the rocks in the pool that you will have to look closely to see them. The park protects their habitat and the habitats of all the creatures within its borders. Want to see more of them? Take a hike!

Hikers in the Smokies can take short walks along creeks or tackle challenging mountain trails that cover many miles.

Check In Why was Great Smoky Mountains National Park established?

GENRE Geography Tour

Read to find out about the wildlife in the Smokies.

A Wildlife Tour of the Smokies

by Sue Miller

Hello, fellow animal lovers, and welcome to Great Smoky Mountains National Park! Our wildlife tour will begin in Cades Cove, a broad valley, or a low area surrounded by mountains. From there, we'll take a quick hop over to the Tremont area to explore some waterfalls. Next, we'll head up to the park's highest point—Clingmans Dome—and we'll end our tour in the Cataloochee Valley. Along the way, we will see amazing wildlife living in its natural environment—the habitats preserved by the national park. Don't forget your binoculars—you don't want to miss a thing.

A buck stands at attention in a meadow in Cades Cove.

Cades Cove

Thanks for getting up so early for our tour around Cades Cove. There's no better time to see the wildlife here than at sunrise or sunset because that's when the animals are most active.

Our first stop is the meadow next to John Oliver's pioneer cabin. A meadow is a grassy area that can occur naturally in forests, but people also can clear trees to make a meadow. Oliver built his house in the early 1800s from trees he cut down.

Look at the white-tailed buck in the meadow keeping a watchful eye on us as he enjoys his morning meal of wildflowers and grass. Can you see his velvet-covered antlers? By late summer, his antlers will be much bigger and the velvet will be gone.

White-tailed deer are not the only wildlife to spot here. The mix of meadow and forest in Cades Cove makes the area an ideal habitat for both gray and red foxes. They can hunt for food in the open meadows, and the trees offer them a good place to hide from animals that hunt them.

River otters were once plentiful in the streams of Cades Cove. In fact, the Cherokee name for this area was "Otter Place." Over the years, they were hunted for their beautiful fur, and this caused them to disappear from Cades Cove. In the 1980s, the park brought some otters back to Cades Cove, and today otters splash and play here once more in nearby Abrams Creek.

A gray treefrog explores a green plant and smiles for the camera.

Tremont

If you like salamanders and frogs, you'll love our next tour stop. Tremont is one of the best places in the park for exploring mountain creeks, so we can search for frogs and salamanders in fast-moving streams, beside waterfalls, under moss-covered rocks, and along forest trails.

Did you know that Great Smoky Mountains National Park is known as the "Salamander Capital of the World"? A whopping five of the world's eight families of salamanders live in the park. Although salamanders look like lizards with smooth, moist skin, they are actually related to frogs. We might see a large, fat hellbender salamander hunting crayfish in a rushing stream. Or maybe we'll spot one of the park's many land salamanders hiding in leaves or under a log.

Keep a watch for frogs along the edge of the streams. Look, there's a gray treefrog peaking around that plant! Let's see if we can find a large bullfrog or some wood frogs.

The Middle Prong of Little River is one of several places in the park where scientists collect information about salamanders and frogs. Some of the scientists are students like you. The Great Smoky Mountains Institute at Tremont runs a citizen scientists program that gives students the opportunity to do hands-on scientific research.

Black bear cubs are very cute, but you should never go near one. Their mothers are always nearby, and they will protect their babies.

Clingmans Dome

Our next stop is Clingmans Dome—the highest peak in the park. Put on a jacket if you have one. At a height of 6,643 feet, the peak, or **summit**, can be 10 to 20 degrees cooler than the surrounding lowlands. The trees at the top of Clingmans Dome are conifers, or trees such as pines, with cones and needle-like leaves. Because it is cold, wet, and very rainy, this forest is classified as a **coniferous rain forest**.

Let's leave the car in the parking lot and trek the rest of the way to the summit on foot. On a clear day like today, you can see 100 miles in all directions from the observation tower. Keep a sharp lookout. The coniferous rain forest is good habitat for black bears, which sometimes wander across the trail. If you see one, don't approach it because bears are dangerous—particularly mother bears with their cubs.

Did you know the black bear is the symbol of the Smokies? There are about 1,500 of them in the park, living on a diet of berries, flowers, nuts, roots, small mammals, and birds. In winter, bears go into a deep sleep, but unlike smaller park animals such as chipmunks and mice, they don't actually **hibernate**. Black bears have been known to wake up quickly if they are disturbed by something or someone trying to enter their dens.

Cataloochee Valley

The Cataloochee Valley is our next stop. Look around. Tall mountain peaks as high as 6,000 feet surround us. Like the meadows of Cades Cove, this valley's open areas are great places to spot different kinds of wildlife.

Late in the day, many animals are out and about. We're likely to see quite a few white-tailed deer, wild turkeys, and a variety of smaller park animals. But what we're really hoping to spot are the magnificent Cataloochee elk.

Once quite common here, elk were overhunted and driven from the area by people before the park was even established. The good news is that the park began a program to reintroduce elk to the area in 2001. Park managers released 25 elk in the Cataloochee Valley that year and another 27 elk in 2002. The herd has slowly grown over time to more than 100 elk.

Elk are large, powerful animals. An average male weighs between 600 and 700 pounds and has antlers that can span five feet! Look at the bull elk standing in the middle of the meadow. He is making the distinctive bugle call he uses to attract a female and warn away other males. He will use his massive antlers to challenge other bull elk.

Cataloochee Valley is the last stop on our wildlife tour. Did you keep track of all the creatures you saw? Which one was your favorite?

In the park, Cataloochee elk can only be found in the Cataloochee Valley.

Check In What are some of the wildlife you will find in Great Smoky Mountains National Park?

GENRE Legend **Read to find out** about the life of Davy Crockett.

Young Davy Crockett

BY ELIZABETH MASSIE

ILLUSTRATED BY DAVID HARRINGTON

Davy Crockett was born and grew up on the Tennessee side of the Great Smoky Mountains. He became an American folk hero—his actions and words became a part of our culture through songs and stories. Sometimes the facts of his life were stretched to make them seem more exciting, but his life really was an adventure!

WHAT A STRONG AND INDEPENDENT BOY! I IMAGINE HE'LL DO GREAT THINGS WHEN HE GROWS UP.
DAVY CROCKETT WAS BORN ON AUGUST 17, 1786, THE FIFTH OF NINE CHILDREN. HE WAS ENERGETIC AND CURIOUS. THE FAMILY LIVED IN A LOG CABIN, WHICH DAVY'S FATHER BUILT WITH HIS OWN HANDS, BY A RIVER IN THE SHADOW OF THE SMOKY MOUNTAINS.
HOLD ON, DAVY, THAT'S NOT A CAT!
EVEN AS A VERY YOUNG CHILD, DAVY LOVED THE OUTDOORS. HE PLAYED IN PUDDLES, CLIMBED TREES, CHASED SKUNKS . . .
NOT IN THE HOUSE!
. . . WADED IN THE CREEK, PICKED BERRIES, AND CAUGHT CRITTERS THAT BELONGED OUTSIDE MORE THAN INSIDE.
8×4=32
10
+5
=15
DAVY'S FAMILY WAS POOR. THEY LIVED SO FAR BACK IN THE WOODS THAT THERE WAS NO SCHOOL NEARBY. THE CHILDREN LEARNED TO READ, WRITE, AND DO ARITHMETIC AT HOME.

JOHN AND REBECCA CROCKETT TAUGHT THEIR CHILDREN WHICH WILD PLANTS WERE SAFE TO EAT, HOW TO AVOID DANGEROUS BEASTS, HOW TO MARK A TRAIL SO THEY DIDN'T GET LOST, AND HOW TO HUNT ANIMALS FOR MEAT AND CLOTHING.
SORRY, DAVY, THERE ISN'T ROOM FOR YOU!
WHEN DAVY WAS FOUR YEARS OLD, HIS OLDER BROTHERS AND A NEIGHBOR BOY NAMED CAMPBELL TOOK THEIR FATHER'S CANOE OUT INTO THE RIVER WITHOUT PERMISSION. DAVY WAS LEFT BEHIND ON THE RIVERBANK.
THE BOYS LOST THE PADDLE AS THE CANOE HEADED STRAIGHT FOR A WATERFALL. A NEIGHBOR DOVE INTO THE RIVER, CAUGHT HOLD OF THE CANOE, AND DRAGGED THE BOYS TO SAFETY.
YOU KIDS NEED TO BE MORE CAREFUL. IF YOU DON'T RESPECT THE RIVER, SHE'LL REACH OUT AND PUNCH YOU!
THAT'S ONE POWERFUL RIVER!

AS DAVY GREW TALLER AND STRONGER, HE HAULED WATER, PLANTED CROPS, WEEDED THE GARDENS, AND HELPED PICK THE VEGETABLES.
WE CAN HELP YOU.
DAVY LEARNED NATURAL REMEDIES FOR SICKNESS AND INJURIES. MANY OF THESE REMEDIES CAME FROM THE CHEROKEE PEOPLE, WHO LIVED IN AND NEAR THE GREAT SMOKY MOUNTAINS.
IN 1794, THE CROCKETTS MOVED SOUTHEAST TO GREENE COUNTY, TENNESSEE. JOHN CROCKETT DECIDED TO BUILD A MILL SO HE COULD EARN A GOOD LIVING GRINDING FARMERS' GRAIN INTO FLOUR.
NATURE SURE GOT US THIS TIME. I HAVE SO MUCH TO LEARN IF I EVER EXPECT TO SURVIVE IN THIS WILDERNESS.
BEFORE THE MILL WAS FINISHED, HOWEVER, A FLOOD WASHED IT AND THE FAMILY'S NEW CABIN AWAY. THIS MADE DAVY RESPECT THE POWER OF NATURE EVEN MORE.

SAFE TRAVELS.
THE CROCKETTS HEADED NORTH AND BUILT A NEW CABIN NEAR THE "GREAT ROAD," WHICH STRETCHED FROM VIRGINIA TO TENNESSEE. PART OF THE CABIN WAS AN INN FOR TRAVELERS ALONG THE GREAT ROAD.
DAVY BECAME ONE OF THE BEST HUNTERS IN THE REGION, PROVIDING MEAT FOR THE INN'S GUESTS AND HIS FAMILY. THOUGH STILL A BOY, HE IMPRESSED ADULT HUNTERS WITH HIS SHARP EYE AND KEEN SENSES OF SIGHT, SMELL, AND HEARING.
BYE, DAVY!
THE WINTER THAT DAVY WAS 12, JOHN CROCKETT HIRED HIM OUT TO JACOB SILER, WHO NEEDED HELP HERDING HIS CATTLE ALONG THE GREAT ROAD FROM TENNESSEE INTO VIRGINIA. DAVY AGREED TO GO IN ORDER TO HELP HIS FAMILY.
DAVY AND MR. SILER COVERED THE 200 MILES TO SILER'S HOME IN TWO WEEKS, THROUGH FREEZING WINDS AND SNOWDRIFTS. DAVY STAYED WITH THE SILERS FOR A WHILE AND THEN HE SET OFF FOR HOME.

AND THEN THERE WAS THE TIME I ESCAPED FROM THREE BIG BLACK BEARS, ALL AT ONCE!
PART OF THE TIME HE WALKED. OTHER TIMES, HE CAUGHT RIDES WITH PEOPLE TRAVELING IN WAGONS OR ON HORSEBACK. HE WAS VERY HAPPY WHEN HE FINALLY SPOTTED HIS FAMILY'S CABIN BY THE GREAT ROAD.
THE YEAR DAVY TURNED 13, HIS FATHER DECIDED HIS SONS SHOULD GO TO SCHOOL TO LEARN HOW TO READ AND WRITE. DAVY DIDN'T LIKE THE IDEA. HE MUCH PREFERRED THE CLASSROOMS OF THE FORESTS, HILLS, AND MOUNTAINS.
THEY'RE NEVER GOING TO CATCH ME. NEVER!
IT DIDN'T TAKE LONG FOR DAVY TO GET IN A FIGHT WITH ANOTHER STUDENT. THEN HE BEGAN SKIPPING CLASSES. WHEN THE SCHOOLMASTER TOLD JOHN CROCKETT THAT DAVY WAS MISSING SCHOOL, DAVY RAN AWAY RATHER THAN FACE HIS FATHER'S ANGER.
HERE, YOUNG MAN. TAKE THIS WITH OUR GOOD WISHES.
THANK YOU VERY MUCH, MA'AM!
DAVY STAYED AWAY FOR TWO-AND-A-HALF YEARS, WORKING AT MANY DIFFERENT JOBS. SOME PEOPLE TOOK ADVANTAGE OF HIM AND STOLE HIS MONEY. OTHER PEOPLE WERE KIND TO HIM AND GAVE HIM A HELPING HAND WHEN HE NEEDED IT.

DAVY! HOW MUCH YOU'VE GROWN. WE MISSED YOU, SON!
DAVY RETURNED HOME TO TENNESSEE WHEN HE WAS 15. HE HAD CHANGED SO MUCH THAT HIS FAMILY DIDN'T RECOGNIZE HIM AT FIRST. HE WENT TO WORK ON A NEARBY FARM TO HELP HIS FATHER PAY DOWN SOME OF HIS DEBTS.
THEN DAVY DECIDED TO GO BACK TO SCHOOL. HE REALIZED THAT BEING ABLE TO READ AND WRITE WOULD BE VERY HELPFUL IN HIS ADULT LIFE.
DAVY FELL IN LOVE WITH POLLY FINLEY, A YOUNG WOMAN WHO LIVED NEARBY. SHE WAS SMART AND PRETTY, AND SHE LOVED BEING OUTSIDE, TOO. THREE DAYS BEFORE DAVY'S NINETEENTH BIRTHDAY, HE AND POLLY WERE MARRIED.
PEOPLE STARTED TO TELL TALL TALES ABOUT HOW DAVY COULD OUTSHOOT, OUTCLIMB, OUTRUN, AND OUTWIT ANY PERSON OR ANIMAL. LIFE WAS GOOD FOR THE RUGGED, INDEPENDENT MAN IN THE COONSKIN CAP.

Check In What qualities did Davy have as a boy that helped him become a folk hero when he grew up?

GENRE Reference Article

Read to find out about the caves that lie under the Smoky Mountains.

LET'S EXPLORE A CAVE

by Catherine Kensington

Did you know there is a world of wonders underneath the Great Smoky Mountains? Over millions of years, water has carved mazes of underground passageways beneath the mountains of the southeastern United States. The people who explore caves are called cavers. Caving can be quite an adventure, but it can be dangerous, too. Cavers must make sure they have the equipment, knowledge, and skill to explore safely.

This caver is exploring Indianapolis Cave, a wild cave in rural Tennessee. There are caves in Great Smoky Mountains National Park, too, and cavers could once explore them. Today, bats that live in these caves are dying from a bat disease called White-Nose Syndrome. The park has closed all of its caves until the disease stops harming bats.

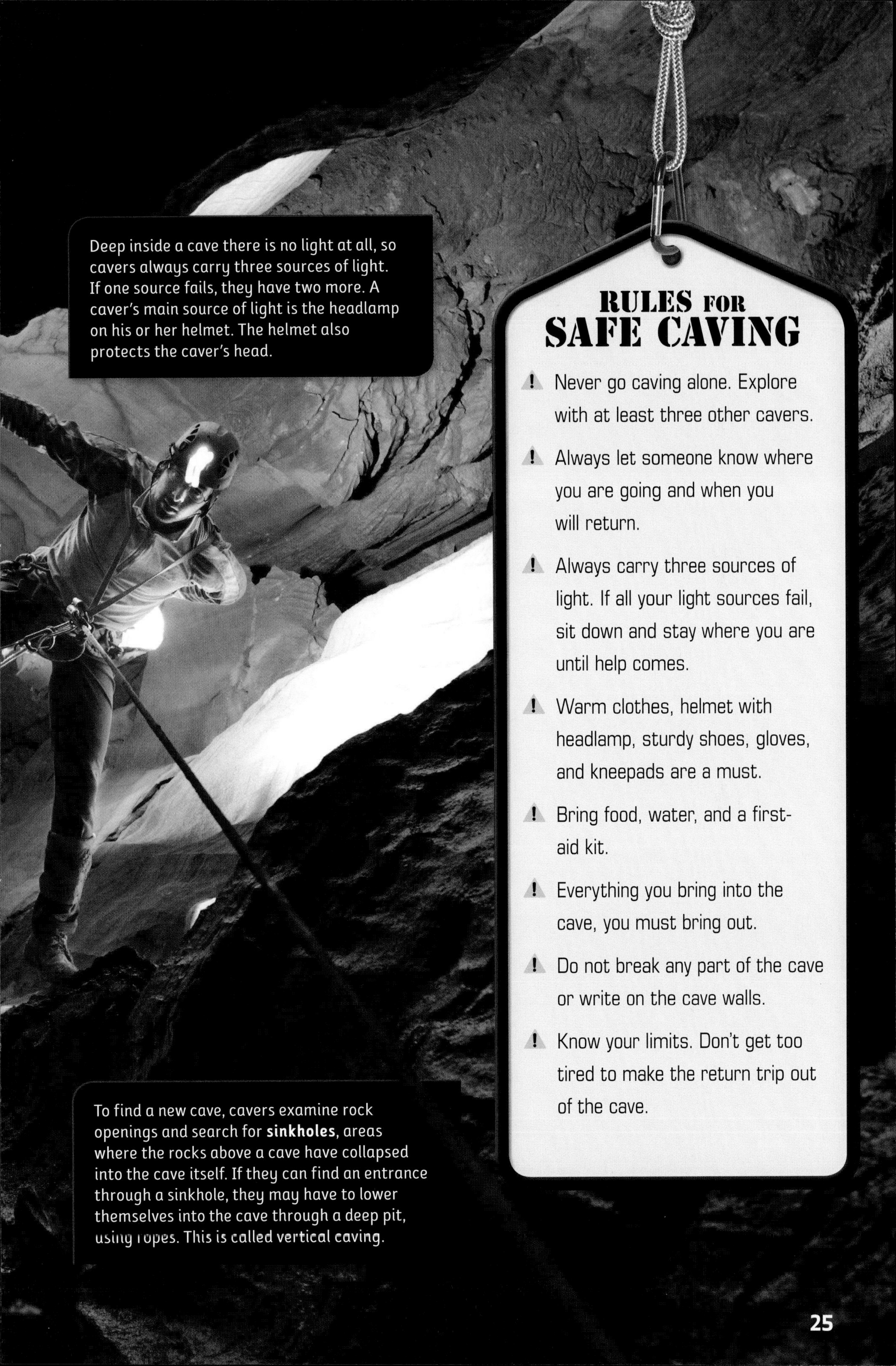

Deep inside a cave there is no light at all, so cavers always carry three sources of light. If one source fails, they have two more. A caver's main source of light is the headlamp on his or her helmet. The helmet also protects the caver's head.

RULES FOR SAFE CAVING

- Never go caving alone. Explore with at least three other cavers.
- Always let someone know where you are going and when you will return.
- Always carry three sources of light. If all your light sources fail, sit down and stay where you are until help comes.
- Warm clothes, helmet with headlamp, sturdy shoes, gloves, and kneepads are a must.
- Bring food, water, and a first-aid kit.
- Everything you bring into the cave, you must bring out.
- Do not break any part of the cave or write on the cave walls.
- Know your limits. Don't get too tired to make the return trip out of the cave.

To find a new cave, cavers examine rock openings and search for **sinkholes**, areas where the rocks above a cave have collapsed into the cave itself. If they can find an entrance through a sinkhole, they may have to lower themselves into the cave through a deep pit, using ropes. This is called vertical caving.

HOW DOES A CAVE FORM?

It seems impossible that raindrops—many trillions of them over hundreds of thousands of years—helped build these cave **formations**, or minerals deposited within a cave. Here's how it happened. Rainwater actually carved the cave out of solid rock. The rock under these mountains can be dissolved, or eaten away, by a mild acid found in rainwater. This forms a cave chamber. When water oozes into a cave, it carries minerals from the soil and rock above and deposits them on the cave's walls, ceiling, and floor. The minerals build up over time and become cave formations. You can see some of them here.

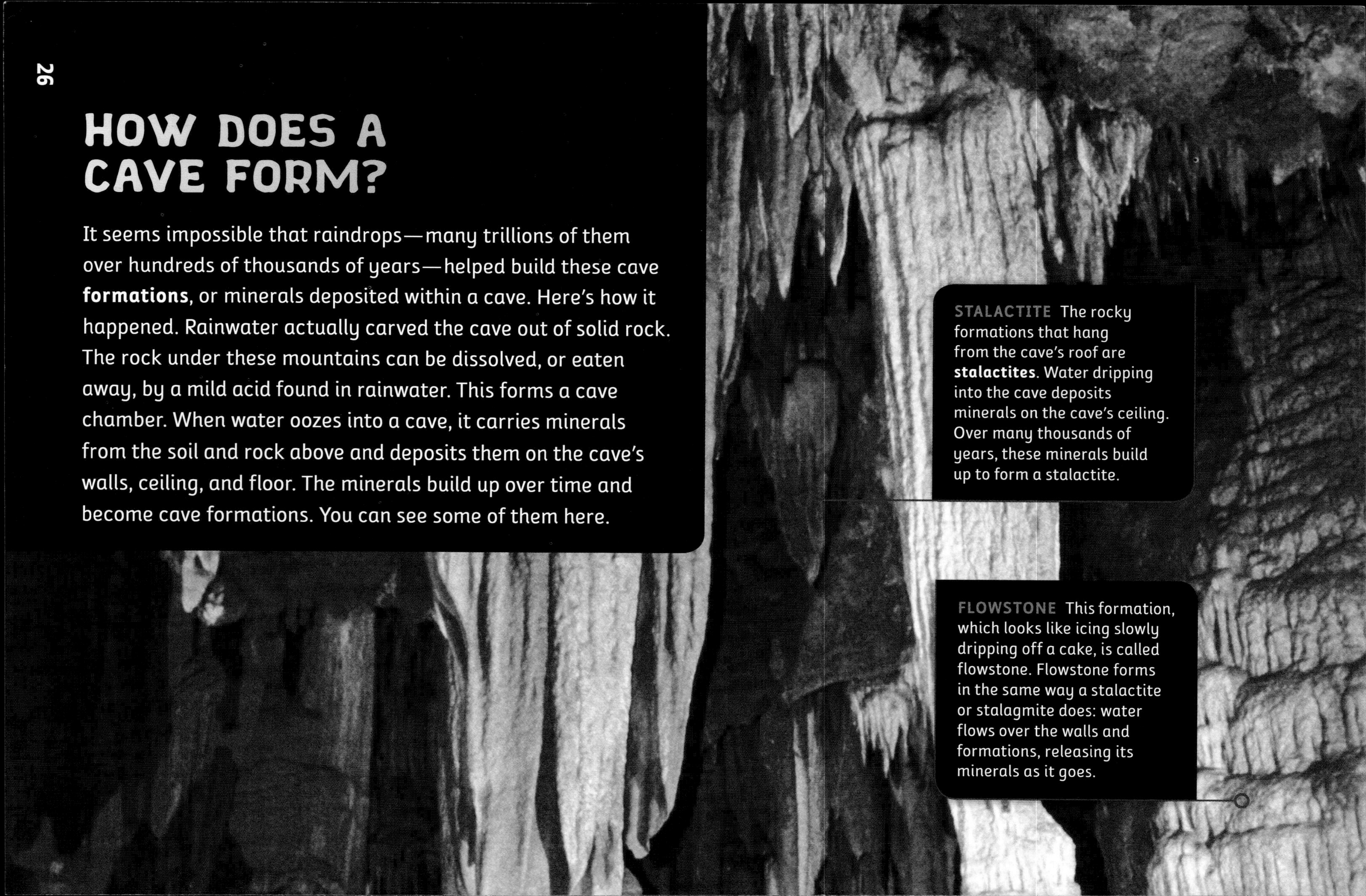

STALAGMITE If dripping water deposits its minerals on the cave floor, over time a **stalagmite** will form. The droplets splash and spread as they hit the floor of the cave, so stalagmites are usually wider and rounder than slender, pointed stalactites.

COLUMN When a stalactite and a stalagmite grow together, they form a column. Once a column forms, the water flowing over it can deposit flowstone on it. That's why some columns can grow to massive size.

HOW A CAVE IS FORMED

Water seeps through the ground and picks up minerals that make it a mild acid. The groundwater enters cracks in the rock and makes them wider.

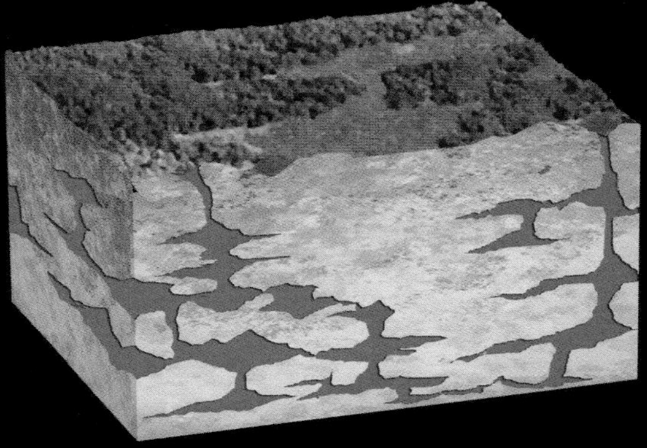

If the cracks become large enough, underground rivers begin to flow through them. The flowing water erodes the rock even more.

If there is air in the cave, droplets of water deposit minerals on the ceiling and floor. Over time, these deposits grow larger to make cave formations.

OPEN TO THE PUBLIC

You don't have to be a caver to visit a cave. There are lots of caves throughout the mountains of the southeastern United States that are open to the public. There was even a public cave in Cades Cove before Great Smoky Mountains National Park was established. In a public cave, walkways, electric lights, steps, and railings have been added to make the cave easy to tour. These caves are cool and damp year-round, so wear a sweater or jacket. If the cave is still changing and growing, you may even get dripped on! Never touch a growing formation, though, because the oil on your hands will keep water from depositing minerals on it. That will stop its growth forever.

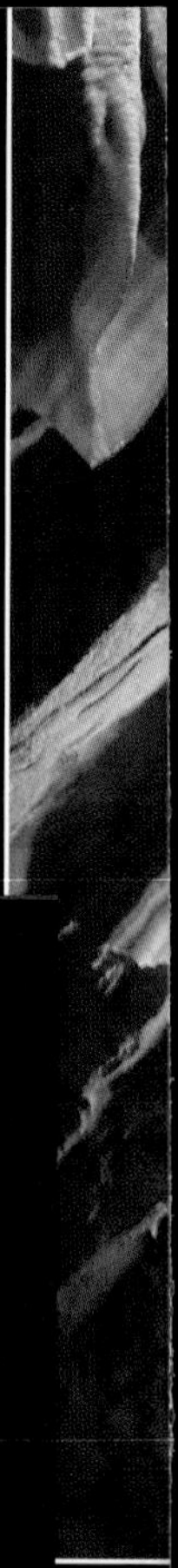

SHENANDOAH CAVERNS Shenandoah Caverns is one of many public caves in Virginia, northeast of the Smokies. This cave was discovered when workers blasted into it as they were building a railroad. Don't these formations look like bacon? Don't try to eat them, though. They are solid rock.

RUBY FALLS This ribbon of falling water is more than 1,000 feet below the surface of Lookout Mountain near Chattanooga, Tennessee. Long ago, water flowed in through a sinkhole and eroded the steep-sided pit where the waterfall is now.

LURAY CAVERNS Luray Caverns is another public cave in Virginia. It has a Stalacpipe Organ! A scientist used cave formations to build this strange musical instrument in the 1950s.The keys of the organ are attached to small, soft mallets that tap formations in the cave so they ring like bells.

TUCKALEECHEE CAVERNS Tuckaleechee Caverns is in Tennessee, very near Great Smoky Mountains National Park. Native Americans and European settlers knew about the cave long ago, but cavers exploring farther into its depths found a huge chamber of magnificent formations. One of the stalagmites is 24 feet tall!

CAVE CRITTERS

Believe it or not, there are creatures that live in caves. Some cave dwellers live near the mouth of a cave, mostly in the "twilight zone" where some light from the outside seeps in. These animals often travel outside the cave to hunt for food and return to the cave for shelter and protection from predators. Other cave creatures live deep beneath the surface where there is no light at all, and they never come out. Long ago, the ancestors of these animals wandered into the cave and stayed. Over thousands of years, their offspring have changed so they can live in a world without light. They are often blind because they do not need to see. Some of them no longer have eyes at all! They also are colorless because they do not need to blend in with their surroundings to fool predators.

CAVE CRICKET Cave crickets have powerful hind legs and long antennae. Some are true cave dwellers, without eyes or color, but most of them leave the cave to search for food. They will eat just about anything as long as they like its smell and are able to chew it.

GRAY BAT When you think about cave creatures, bats probably come to mind. Many types of bats roost in caves during the day and fly out of their caves each evening to hunt. An average bat colony has up to 25,000 members! Bats eat insects such as mosquitoes and keep them from becoming too plentiful.

CAVE CRAYFISH These colorless, eyeless crayfish live in deep cave pools and streams where there is no light, ever. They feed on tiny pieces of leaves that flow into the cave from the surface. Since underground streams bring food to them, cave crayfish can starve when a drought dries up the water supply.

CAVE SALAMANDERS Many different types of salamanders live in caves. This one lives in the "twilight zone" and ventures out of the cave at night to hunt for food. It has a long tongue that it shoots out to capture prey such as insects, worms, and even smaller salamanders.

Check In How did caves form in and around the Great Smoky Mountains?

Discuss

1. What ideas do you think connect the four selections you read in this book? Explain.

2. Which stop on the Smoky Mountain wildlife tour would you most like to visit in person? Why?

3. How does an American hero such as Davy Crockett compare to superheroes in movies? How are they similar and different?

4. How are the caves underneath the Smoky Mountains different from the land above them? How are they similar?

5. What do you still wonder about Great Smoky Mountains National Park? How can you learn more?